● ●

HERE'S A PIECE OF A REAL-LIFE INTER-
VIEW WITH ONE OF THE *GHOSTWRITER*
GUYS *OFF* THE SET. CAN YOU TELL
WHICH ONE HE PLAYS ON THE SET?

When it comes to most things, Sheldon is very
confident. But two things get him a little nervous:
swimming in deep water and talking to girls.

But, as Ghostwriter might say, sometimes the
best way to conquer a fear is to face it. Sheldon
says this about talking to girls: "I might be nervous when I'm doing it, but I'll do it. Maybe it's
not my strong suit, but if I see something I want,
I go for it. Otherwise I'll feel like I let myself
down."

Sheldon likes girls who are smart and have a
sense of humor. He likes girls who look good, too.

People who aren't willing to question and think
about things probably won't become Sheldon's
friends. "I don't like people who stereotype," he
says. "I don't like people who won't look beyond
the surface."

JOIN THE TEAM!

Do you watch GHOSTWRITER on PBS? Then you know that when you read and write to solve a mystery or unravel a puzzle, you're using the same smarts and skills the Ghostwriter team uses.

We hope you'll join the team and read along to help solve the mysterious and puzzling goings-on in these GHOSTWRITER books!

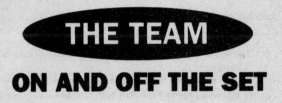

THE TEAM

ON AND OFF THE SET

BY
JOY DUCKETT CAIN

BANTAM BOOKS
NEW YORK • TORONTO • LONDON • SYDNEY • AUCKLAND

THE TEAM: ON AND OFF THE SET

A Bantam Book / September 1993

Art direction by Marva Martin
Cover design by Susan Herr
Book design by Patrice Fodero

ISBN 0-553-56455-2

Published simultaneously in the United States and Canada

Bantam Books are published by Bantam Books, a division of Bantam
Doubleday Dell Publishing Group, Inc. Its trademark, consisting of the
words "Bantam Books" and the portrayal of a rooster, is Registered in U.S.
Patent and Trademark Office and in other countries. Marca Registrada.
Bantam Books, 1540 Broadway, New York, New York 10036.

PRINTED IN THE UNITED STATES OF AMERICA

OPM   0   9 8 7 6 5 4 3 2 1

Zap! Crash! Blam! The air is filled with the sounds of fireballs and pounding fists. Rainbows of light flicker on tense faces.

"Aaagh! That was my last life!" someone wails.

Welcome to the Power Video Arcade—a great place to hang. Kids are everywhere. There are lots of games—X-Men, Robotron, Funkey Shoot—as well as a soccer table game. A sign on the wall says:

DOUBLE DEFENDERS TOURNAMENT
SATURDAY, SEPT. 13
12 NOON

The front door swings open. Jamal, Lenni, Gaby, and Alex—kids on the Ghostwriter team—stride in. A group of kids is behind them. They look angry. They head straight for four other kids at a video game.

A little girl in the group suddenly shrieks. "That's him!" she yells, pointing at one of the game players. "He's the one who stole my backpack."

"We want our money back, THABTOS!" Gaby says.

The four kids at the game look nervously at one another. One of them tries to walk away, but Jamal steps in front of him. The two boys stare at each other.

Suddenly a man's voice breaks the tense silence. "Cut! Okay, let's see what this looks like on camera."

Welcome to the behind-the-scenes world of *Ghostwriter*!

In television nothing is really as it seems. Remember the video arcade in the scene above? It's really a set in a studio in New York City. A set is something that's built to *look* like a real place, but it's not real. There are living room, kitchen, and bedroom sets right near the arcade set.

Remember the angry kids? They're all actors: Gaby's real name is Mayteana Morales, and Jamal's is Sheldon Turnipseed. What they do may look easy if you're watching it on television, but many hours of hard work go into each show. The actors have to memorize lines, rehearse, and learn their staging (where they're supposed to stand on the set) before they actually tape a scene. Often they must say the same lines over and over during rehearsals. Then they do it over and over again for the taping. It's a long, tiring process.

And the actors are just one part of the process. You'd be surprised at how many people it takes to bring the *Ghostwriter* television show to you. For instance, before the actors can learn their lines, writers have to write a script. Set designers have to make the sets. Details must be taken care of: An actor can't take milk out of the refrigerator in a scene unless someone first puts the milk *into* the refrigerator, right? Prop people take care of things like that. Then there are makeup, wardrobe, and hair people, camera people, boom operators who work the microphones—and more!

But since the actors are the ones everyone sees, they're the ones everyone wants to know. This book will introduce you to the main actors on *Ghostwriter* and tell you about what their real lives are like. For example, one actor almost drowned on a family vacation. And one actress has a twin sister. Who are they? Read on and find out!

Oh, one more thing. Don't be surprised if a special guest shows up in the following pages. This guest loves to read and communicate through writing. His initials are G.W., and chances are he'll bring some of his friends along, too.

So are you ready to experience *Ghostwriter* in a completely different way? The fun is about to begin!

HELLO, READER.

MY FRIENDS CALL ME GHOST-WRITER. I DON'T KNOW MY REAL NAME. I DON'T EVEN KNOW WHERE I CAME FROM. ALL I KNOW IS THAT FOR MANY YEARS I WAS ASLEEP IN THE PAGES OF AN OLD BOOK IN JA-MAL JENKINS'S BASEMENT. THEN ONE DAY JAMAL FOUND THE BOOK AND I WOKE UP. I WAS AFRAID. I COULDN'T SEE OR HEAR OR EVEN TALK. I DIDN'T REMEMBER ANY-THING. I DIDN'T KNOW WHERE I WAS OR WHAT HAD HAPPENED TO ME. MOST OF ALL, I WAS LONELY.

BUT I COULD FEEL JAMAL'S PRES-ENCE. HE HAD A MACHINE FULL OF WORDS AND LETTERS—A COMPUT-

ER. I USED THE LETTERS IN IT TO WRITE TO HIM. THOUGH HE WAS FRIGHTENED TO RECEIVE A MESSAGE FROM OUT OF NOWHERE, AFTER A WHILE HE WROTE BACK TO ME. HE HAS BEEN A TRUE FRIEND EVER SINCE.

NOW WE TRY TO HELP EACH OTHER, AS FRIENDS DO. JAMAL AND SOME OTHER FRIENDS—MEMBERS OF THE GHOSTWRITER TEAM—ARE HELPING ME DISCOVER WHO I AM. AND WHENEVER THE GHOSTWRITER TEAM NEEDS ME, I TRY TO HELP THEM, TOO. IF YOU'D LIKE TO MEET THE MEMBERS OF THE TEAM, JUST KEEP READING. I'LL BE CONTACTING EACH ONE OF THEM—STARTING WITH JAMAL, MY FIRST FRIEND.

JAMAL JENKINS

GW: HELLO, JAMAL.

JAMAL: Hey Ghostwriter! What's up? I was just getting ready to practice my karate. The *sensei* at the youth center is a black belt—that's the top rank in karate. One day I'll be one, too. At least I want to be. But it takes a lot of hard work.

GW: YOU'LL MAKE IT IF YOU KEEP TRYING.

JAMAL: Yeah, I know: Try. Grandma CeCe always says, "If at first you don't succeed, try, try again." Hey, I'm not going to quit or anything—I'm not a quitter, you know—but I wish karate could be easier.

GW: THINGS THAT ARE WORTHWHILE AREN'T ALWAYS EASY.

JAMAL: Tell me about it. Do you know what my mom's doing? She's going to school. *Again.* I don't really get it. She already has her college degree, and she's a nurse. That's a good job, right? But now she's going to school in the evenings after work so she can get her master's degree. I *know* it's not easy, because she always has a ton of books to read or papers to do. But to her all this schooling is worthwhile.

Don't get me wrong: I like school okay. I love to read. And I'm proud of my mom. But after I graduate from college, I don't think you'll see me rushing to go back again. Uh-uh. Once will be quite enough.

GW: ISN'T YOUR SISTER IN COLLEGE, TOO?

JAMAL: Yeah, Danitra goes to the University of Pennsylvania. She lives on campus. She gave me her computer before she left. Man, it's great! I can play video games on it and write reports on it—and, of course, talk to you on it, Ghostwriter.

But you know what? With Danitra gone, it's been awfully quiet in this house. Just me and Mom and Dad and Grandma CeCe. It's funny. When Danitra was here, I couldn't wait for her to go to college. You know how big sisters can be—they'll get on your last nerve if you let them. But now I kind of miss her. Sometimes we'd have these long conversations, just the two of us. She wasn't all bad. Just don't tell her I said that.

GW: OF COURSE NOT. YOU CAN TRUST ME.

JAMAL: I know.

GW: IS SOMETHING WRONG? YOU SEEM PENSIVE.

JAMAL: Pensive?

GW: THOUGHTFUL. AS IF SOMETHING SAD IS ON YOUR MIND.

JAMAL: Well . . . something *is* on my mind. Have you talked to Rob lately?

GW: NO. IS EVERYTHING ALL RIGHT? IS HE IN TROUBLE?

JAMAL: No, no, it's nothing like that. See, about a week ago Momo Morris let me borrow his Walkman tape player. My grandma knows that I like Boyz II Men—they're a band—so when she saw their new tape on sale, she got it for me. But she forgot that my tape player has been broken for nearly a month. So I had this great tape but nothing to listen to it on. Anyway, that's why Momo let me borrow *his* tape player.

GW: WHAT'S A TAPE PLAYER?

JAMAL: Oh, sorry. I always forget you don't know about all these modern machines. Remember when I told you about television? How a television is this big box that lets you see *and* hear people? Well, with a tape player you can only hear people—so tapes are great for recording music on. But you can't listen to your tape unless you have a tape player. They make portable ones that come with headphones that go over your ears. The whole thing is so small you can carry it with you in your jacket or bookbag.

GW: SO YOU CAN TRAVEL WITH MUSIC PLAYING IN YOUR EARS? MY GOODNESS!

JAMAL: Yeah, it's cool. But it can also be dangerous.

GW: HOW?

JAMAL: Well, like I said, Momo let me borrow his Walkman. Dad needed some nails for this shelf he's building in the basement, so I was listening to my new tape on the Walkman as I headed for the hardware store.

GW: SO FAR THAT DOESN'T SOUND DANGEROUS.

JAMAL: That's just when Rob came up behind me on his skateboard. It was an accident: Rob yelled that he'd race me to the corner, but I didn't hear him. I didn't even know he was behind me, because I was listening to my tape. So Rob thought I was going to run straight down the block and suddenly I cut in front of him to go into the hardware store.

GW: DANGEROUS.

JAMAL: And painful. We crashed into each other and both of us fell to the ground. Fortunately, we survived. Unfortunately, the Walkman didn't.

GW: I SEE.

JAMAL: When Momo heard what happened, he was ready to fight Rob. According to Momo, Rob did it on purpose.

GW: THAT COULDN'T BE TRUE.

JAMAL: No, of course not. It really *was* an accident. But sometimes Momo and Rob just don't see eye to eye. Momo's got this real tough attitude, you know. And Rob does, too, in his own way. But then we sat down and talked. I told Momo that Rob really didn't mean to do it and that the accident was as much my fault as it was Rob's. It took a while, but eventually Momo calmed down. Especially after Rob and I agreed to split the cost of buying him a new Walkman.

GW: THAT'S GOOD.

JAMAL: Yeah, but it would be even better if I had some money. Oh, well, I'll get it somehow. Maybe Dad will pay me to do some extra chores around the house.

GW: MAYBE YOU COULD GO TO YOUR FATHER'S JOB AND HELP HIM OUT THERE.

JAMAL: Nah, I don't think so. Dad works for the New York City subway system; he's in the control center. He's sort of like a traffic cop for the train system. They don't let kids mess around with stuff like that.

GW: A SUBWAY IS AN UNDERGROUND TRAIN, RIGHT?

JAMAL: That's right. When Dad was younger, though, he used to be a railroad conductor. He traveled all over the country, just like his grandfather did. Great-grandpa Ezra was a sleeping-car porter. He helped form a union to make life better for other porters. He even lost a pinky finger doing his job for the union.

GW: HE MUST HAVE BEEN VERY BRAVE.

JAMAL: Word.

GW: WHAT WORD?

JAMAL: No, Ghostwriter—"word" is slang. It means "really" or "yes."

GW: OH, I GET IT.

JAMAL: But you're right, Ezra must have been something else. I hope I can always stick up for things I believe in just the way he did.

GW: YOU ALREADY DO.

JAMAL: You really think so?

GW: WORD.

JAMAL: All right, Ghostwriter! Soon you'll know all the new expressions better than I do! Oops, my grandma's calling me. It's dinnertime; I've got to go. Later!

SHELDON TURNIPSEED

One day Sheldon Turnipseed (who plays Jamal) was watching television when a show about children and acting came on. Sheldon was fascinated. Acting looked like fun! Sheldon immediately told his mother that he had to try acting. He knew what he wanted. After all, he was six years old!

At first his mother didn't pay much attention. She thought Sheldon would forget about acting and want to try something else instead. But he didn't. So Mrs. Turnipseed finally agreed to help her son get started. Sheldon's been in the acting business ever since.

That story tells a lot about Sheldon. It shows that he's persistent; he'll keep after something until he gets it. And it shows that he's curious.

Most of all, it shows that Sheldon isn't afraid

to try new things. "I think it's very important to go out and experience things, as opposed to staying in one spot all the time," he says. "I think you should get out."

Sheldon got his get-up-and-go attitude from his parents. Like Jamal, Sheldon lives in Brooklyn, New York. Sheldon's mom, Juanita, is an elementary-school teacher. His dad, Alfred, is an insurance agent.

All Sheldon's life, his parents have taken him, his older brother, Alfred, and his older sister, Erica, to parks, museums, and plays. Mr. and Mrs. Turnipseed wanted Alfred, Erica, and Sheldon to see all the things that New York City had to offer. They believed that the more their children saw, the more things they'd want to learn about.

The Turnipseeds were right. Today Alfred and Erica are both in college. Sheldon himself goes to the Bronx High School of Science, which is one of the top public schools in New York City. Most days Sheldon has a private teacher, or tutor, on the *Ghostwriter* set. But when the show has a "dark" week (that's when the actors aren't working), Sheldon goes back to his regular school. It's not an easy schedule. But so far he's doing just fine.

Before working on *Ghostwriter* Sheldon had small movie roles. Two of the pictures he was in were *Mo' Better Blues* and *Jungle Fever*. The director of both films was Spike Lee. Sheldon watched Lee as he worked and he liked what he saw. "He's a no-nonsense type of guy," Sheldon says.

Since Sheldon is also interested in what goes on behind the camera, he may want to become a director like Lee when he grows up. Sheldon is thinking about studying filmmaking when he gets to college.

But first he has to finish high school. Some of his favorite subjects are current events, American history, and Greek and Roman history. He also likes English literature. "But not grammar," Sheldon says. "I *don't* like grammar."

Sheldon does well in school, but it would be a big mistake to think that he's only into books. No way! Although he doesn't care for what he calls "the big three" (baseball, basketball, and football), he does like cycling, skiing, and ice skating a lot. "Anything that involves speed," he says.

One particular skiing adventure stands out in Sheldon's mind. "I was coming down the slope at, like, fifty-five miles per hour, and when I went into my tuck position, I heard this rattling noise," he says. He looked down and saw that one of his skis was coming off! "I'm, like, 'Oh, that's nice!' I was coming to a spot where you kind of have to jump off and I wondered how was I going to do it. All of this took place in two seconds, but it seemed like a lifetime to me."

Sheldon's only choice was to fall down. "I remember just lying in the snow, looking at one ski way over there and the pole way over the other way and thinking how great that was. Speed! It was just so beautiful. Then I just got up and picked up my skis and went back down the rest of the way."

Sheldon's all-time favorite sport is karate. Like Jamal on *Ghostwriter,* he's working for the top rank—the black belt. He likes karate because it makes him use his mind *and* his body. It gives him confidence, too. "I don't go looking for trouble, like some people do, but I'm prepared for trouble," he says.

Let's see: Both Sheldon and Jamal, the character he plays, love karate and live in Brooklyn. What else do they have in common?

"He's a little bit stubborn and I'm a little bit stubborn," Sheldon admits. "But also Jamal's very just and honest. These are things I like about him . . . and that are similar to me, too." He laughs.

Sheldon likes to read—he especially loves stories about knights who lived a long time ago. Knights were soldiers during the Middle Ages.

He also likes to draw. Sometimes he'll draw landscapes. Other times he'll draw portraits. One of Sheldon's favorite works is a picture he drew a few years ago of two knights fighting on horseback. It now hangs on his bedroom wall, not far away from a photograph of Dr. Martin Luther King, Jr.

Sheldon likes to share his artwork with his friends. Since they met on *Ghostwriter*, David Lopez, who plays Alex, has become good buddies with Sheldon. They hang out on the set together and help each other memorize lines. They work together with a teacher on the set. They even sleep over at each other's house.

"Sheldon drew a nice picture of me and him," David says. "It was a picture of us in suits and wearing sunglasses. Then Sheldon cut out a picture of a car—a Viper—and put it in the background. That was cool." So cool that David now has that picture hanging on the wall in *his* bedroom.

On Sheldon's bedroom wall are pictures of more cars, a Lamborghini and a Ferrari. Sheldon loves cars. He wants to get a Porsche—but first he has to get a driver's license!

When it comes to most things, Sheldon is very confident. But two things get him nervous: swimming in deep water and talking to girls.

But, as Ghostwriter might say, sometimes the best way to conquer a fear is to face it. Sheldon says this about talking to girls: "I might be nervous when I'm doing it, but I'll do it. Maybe it's not my strong suit, but if I see something I want, I go for it. Otherwise I'll feel like I let myself down."

Sheldon likes girls who are smart and have a sense of humor. He likes girls who look good, too.

People who aren't willing to question and think

about things probably won't become Sheldon's friends. "I don't like people who stereotype," he says. "I don't like people who won't look beyond the surface."

When Sheldon hangs out, it's usually with the guys. He has about ten close friends. Four of those guys are superclose buddies. Most of them go to the same school Sheldon does.

When Sheldon and the guys get together, they sometimes meet at a library to work on a project. From there they may go to Greenwich Village. The Village is a section of New York City that has lots of cool stores. Then Sheldon and his friends may go to a movie or a restaurant. Sometimes they'll go to a party. That's one of Sheldon's favorite things to do.

But even if they do nothing at all, Sheldon says, that's cool, too. "Basically, the perfect day for me is not where I am but who I'm with," he says. "Because I could be in my house all day, but if I have my friends with me, it would be a nice day."

MUSIC IS THE WAY LENNI FRAZIER SAYS WHAT'S ON HER MIND. WHEN I FIRST FOUND HER, SHE WAS WRITING A SONG. THIS IS HOW IT WENT:

GROWN-UPS SAY THE WORLD NEEDS CHANGING.
THEY SAY "MAYBE SOMEDAY." IT'S NOT UP TO THEM.
IT'S UP TO US, WE GOTTA SHOW 'EM THE WAY.

IF ANYONE CAN SHOW THE WAY, IT'S LENNI. SHE MAY HAVE A HARD TIME SAYING WHAT SHE MEANS IN SCHOOL ESSAYS, BUT HER RAPS AND SONGS GET RIGHT TO THE POINT. AND THEY HAVE A BEAT THAT WILL MAKE YOU MOVE!

LENNI FRAZIER

GW: HELLO, LENNI.

LENNI: Hey, Ghostwriter! I was thinking about you.

GW: REALLY?

LENNI: Yeah! I haven't talked to you in a while. Where have you been hiding?

GW: WHERE YOU CAN'T FIND ME.

LENNI: Ha, ha. Very funny. But I'll tell you, I could use a laugh right now. This social studies assignment just isn't happening. We have to write a paper about a significant event that occurred in the 1960s.

GW: AND YOU DON'T KNOW MUCH ABOUT THIS TIME PERIOD?

LENNI: Oh, I know a lot about the 1960s. My dad talks about those days all the time. Let's see:

Toward the beginning of the sixties, the Vietnam War was building up. And in 1969 the U.S. landed the first man on the moon. His name was Neil Armstrong. And in the middle of the decade Dr. Martin Luther King, Jr., led the civil-rights struggle. That was a fight to get equal rights for African Americans.

GW: IT SOUNDS AS IF THERE WAS A LOT GOING ON!

LENNI: Yeah. My dad says the sixties were really something. And some of the people back then were pretty cool, too. Once, Dad did this show in the Village to aid homeless people—

GW: HOMELESS? LIKE ROB'S FRIEND DOUBLE T?

LENNI: Exactly. See, there are lots of homeless people. They live . . . outside. Some live on park benches. Others live in alleyways or empty lots. Many have cardboard boxes to protect them from the rain. The boxes are their homes. It's really sad.

GW: WHY DON'T PEOPLE WITH HOMES HELP THEM?

LENNI: Some people try to. Like my dad. See, this particular gig—or show—that he did was to benefit the homeless. All of the money they made from the show went to the homeless. And lots of stars from the 1960s performed at that show. Boy, were they cool. I met Bob Dylan there and Richie Havens. It was great. Now if only my social studies paper could be half as great!

GW: WHAT'S THE PROBLEM?

LENNI: The *paper* is the problem. Writing the paper. I mean, you know I love to write songs. But writing papers is different, because you have to spell words correctly. And your sentences have to have the proper punctuation. And you have to make paragraphs and use the right words and stuff. It involves—yuck—English! Ooh, I hate to write papers!

GW: BUT YOU'RE WRITING NOW.

LENNI: This is different; I mean, this is fun. There's no pressure. Did I ever tell you about what happened to me last year in Mr. Miller's class?

GW: I DON'T THINK SO.

LENNI: It's not a pretty story. Mr. Miller took over for our regular teacher when she got sick. He was really big on grammar. He wanted us to learn the parts of speech.

GW: LIKE NOUNS AND VERBS?

LENNI: Right, and pronouns and adjectives—the whole shebang. Mr. Miller said he'd give a test on the parts of speech at the end of the term and that our score on the test would be ninety percent of our final grade.

GW: HOW DID YOU DO? DID YOU STUDY?

LENNI: Did I study? *Did I study?* Ghostwriter, I studied so much that my brain hurt. I studied so much that my dad thought he had the wrong daughter. I studied so much even *I* began to worry about myself! And after all those weeks of studying, when Mr. Miller put that test paper in front of me, my brain just went numb. It was an ice cube.

GW: WHAT GRADE DID YOU GET?

LENNI: A 71. Two weeks of studying and I get a lousy 71. I tell you, I'm no good at this stuff.

GW: PERHAPS IT'S ALL IN YOUR HEAD.

LENNI: So what are you saying? That I need to see a doctor or something?

GW: NO. MAYBE YOU SHOULD RELAX A LITTLE, THOUGH.

LENNI: When pigs fly!

GW: BUT PIGS DON'T FLY.

LENNI: Exactly. I don't think I'll *ever* be able to relax where schoolwork is concerned. Not until pigs fly. That's a saying my mom used to use.

GW: DO YOU REMEMBER MUCH ABOUT YOUR MOTHER?

LENNI: Some. Like, Mommy used to do "knock knock" jokes with me. Hey, let's do one together! When I say "Knock knock," you say "Who's there?" Okay?

GW: OKAY.

LENNI: Knock knock.

GW: WHO'S THERE?

LENNI: Banana.

GW: COME IN.

LENNI: No, Ghostwriter. You want to find out more about Banana, so you're supposed to ask "Banana who?"

GW: OH. BANANA WHO?

LENNI: Knock knock.

GW: WHO'S THERE?

LENNI: Banana.

GW: BANANA WHO?

LENNI: Knock knock.

GW: WHO'S THERE?

LENNI: Orange.

GW: ORANGE WHO?

LENNI: Orange you glad I didn't say banana again?

GW: HA, HA. VERY FUNNY!

LENNI: Yeah, Mommy loved corny stuff like that, too.

GW: WHAT ELSE DO YOU REMEMBER ABOUT HER?

LENNI: Well, she made some mean macaroni and cheese. And she always smelled nice. I used to love going into the bathroom right after she took a bubble bath, because the air was warm and smelled so sweet.

You know, sometimes I get scared because I'm beginning to forget things about her. She died when I was seven; that's a long time ago.

GW: IF SHE'S IN YOUR HEART, SHE IS NEVER FAR AWAY.

LENNI: So Mommy's right here with me? I like that.

Hey, all *right*! Guess what? Dad just walked in the door. I thought he'd be home a lot later than this. And I smell pizza! I'd love to hang and talk some more, Ghostwriter, but I'm starved. Catch you later—I'm outta here!

BLAZE BERDAHL

Blaze Berdahl (who plays Lenni) comes from an acting family. Her father, Roger, has acted on Broadway. Her older brother, Sky, has done commercials, Broadway shows, and movies. Her sister, Beau, has done commercials, a movie, and a Broadway show. In a way even Blaze's mother, Rita, is a part of show business. Mrs. Berdahl used to work as a social worker and a substitute teacher, but these days she spends so much time taking her children to and from auditions, she could be considered an "honorary" actor, too.

So what does Blaze want to do when she grows up?

"I want to be a psychologist," she says. "I like listening to people's problems, maybe helping them. There are so many different problems in the world today that sometimes you kind of feel guilty when you can't help someone—like one of your friends."

Friends are important to Blaze. Although she likes working on *Ghostwriter,* some things in her life have changed since she got that job. Blaze misses going to school with her best friend, Julie. In fact, she misses a lot about "regular" school: the kids, her teacher, the auditorium, the gym. She even misses playing "keep away" in the schoolyard.

Still, Blaze says there's a good side to show business. "I like acting because you get to meet a lot of nice people," she says. "Sometimes it's surprising to think you could ever be like them. It's kind of cool."

But guess what's even cooler: having a twin! Beau is not only Blaze's twin sister—she and Blaze are *identical* twins. Imagine how much fun that must be! Yet even though they look alike, Blaze and Beau are very different. For instance, Beau is a little bit tomboy and Blaze is a little bit preppy. Beau loves the color black while Blaze adores purple. Beau likes wearing sweatpants and sneakers, but Blaze has been known to put on skirts and dress shoes. The list goes on and on.

Both girls have been in show business all their lives. When Blaze was an infant, she did some baby wipes commercials. Naturally, she doesn't remember them. By the time she was about three years old, though, she was forced to retire. Why? Well, Blaze didn't have much hair. She looked like a boy. That's not good for a little girl in show business. Thank goodness Blaze's hair grew in!

The word *blaze* means a flame or a strongly burning fire. You wouldn't think of a fire as being timid or shy, would you? Well, neither is Blaze Berdahl. At least not most of the time.

"When I was in kindergarten, my teacher would put on these *Pete's Dragon* records and I would sing at naptime," Blaze says. "I wasn't very good back then, but I'd be shouting and belting it out. I'm only shy, actually, for people that I know and like. Like my family: I don't want to sing for my family; I don't want to sing for my relatives. I just want to sing for people I don't know. Like, I wouldn't be shy in a Broadway show or anything like that, but I would be shy singing for my family at a dinner. I don't know why."

Blaze has appeared in many plays. She says that she likes being in plays just as much as she likes doing movies or television, but that being onstage is harder. "In plays you have to memorize all your lines at one time. But in something like *Ghostwriter* or in a movie, where they don't shoot the whole story all at once, you can memorize scenes at different times," says Blaze. "It's not as hard. In plays you have to concentrate a lot."

But there's an instant reward that comes with being onstage. "Hearing the applause makes you feel great," she admits.

One of Blaze's first big parts was in a Stephen King movie called *Pet Sematary*. This scary movie was about pets that came back from the dead. And even though Blaze saw the fake animals and dummies that were used while the film was being made, that didn't help much when she sat in the movie theater. "When I actually saw the movie, there were scenes that I didn't see them do and I was scared," Blaze admits. "Actually, in the middle of the movie I had to be excused to go to the rest room so that I could skip some of the scary parts."

Her part in *Ghostwriter* is nowhere near as frightening. Although both Blaze and Lenni are pretty outspoken, Blaze thinks there's a big difference between them. "Lenni's kind of blunt, kind of rude sometimes. She's really upfront with her friends. She tells them if they have a tacky dress on or something," says Blaze. "I wouldn't do that. I'm really not like Lenni. She's kind of cool, though. I like her. And some of her outfits are pretty cool, too."

Although Blaze will occasionally wear dresses or skirts, she usually wears casual clothes. But not *too* casual. "I'm not the kind of person who would wear sweatpants or anything like that," she explains.

But she *is* the type of person who likes to browse around bath and body shops. These shops sell scented lotions and soaps. That's right up Blaze's alley, because she collects perfumes and perfume bottles. Right now Blaze has about thirteen perfume bottles at home, including three crystal ones. Her favorite perfumes are Lauren and Chanel No. 5.

If you want to hang out with Blaze, you'd better be ready to bowl! Blaze likes bowling a lot.

She also likes skiing and ice skating as well as gymnastics and tap dancing. When it comes to reading, she stays away from books that start off boring. And if you really want to make her happy, give her a book that will make her cry. *Where the Red Fern Grows,* by Wilson Rawls, is one of her all-time favorites, even though she read it way back in the fourth grade.

Blaze and her family live in Manhattan in a three-bedroom apartment. A very *large* three-bedroom apartment. It has to be. Besides Blaze, her parents, and her brother and sister, the Berdahls have two turtles and eight cats. Yes, eight cats. Blaze's favorite is Raifie, a black cat with greenish-yellow eyes. Raifie was adopted from an animal shelter. She was named after another cat that Blaze's parents owned long before Blaze was born.

Sometimes it's hard to tell who's in charge at Blaze's house, the people or the cats. "They sleep everywhere," she says. "They sleep on my bed, in the living room, on the table, on top of the TV. And the funny thing is we buy them beds and stuff, but they'll sleep anywhere *but* in their beds."

Blaze's bedroom is pink and white. She has lots

of cupids and hearts and bows and teddy bears on her wall—"things that look cute." Right outside her room is a small terrace. It used to be junky, with lots of boxes on it, but Blaze and her father cleaned it. Now Blaze grows azaleas, roses, and ivy out there.

Blaze is the baby of the family, since Sky is the oldest and Beau was born a minute before she was. But she thinks of herself as a twin. And being a twin can be fun. "When we were younger, we annoyed a lot of people," says Blaze. For example, if their aunts came to visit, "we'd go upstairs and switch clothes. Then they'd be really confused." But Blaze says that she and Beau never switched classes at school. And even though they fight sometimes—especially about wearing each other's clothes—they like each other a lot.

"When my sister went to California to rehearse for a play, I realized that I was really bored being the only twin in the house," Blaze says. She couldn't wait for Beau to come back home.

So what's the best part about being a twin? Blaze grins. Easy question. "There's always some-one around that you can play with!"

ALEX FERNANDEZ, LOVER OF MYS-
TERIES! ALEX IS A MASTER AT
CRACKING CODES, TRACKING SUS-
PECTS, AND COLLECTING CLUES.

ALEX WILL NEVER BE BORED. HE
FINDS EXCITEMENT EVERYWHERE:
IN LIFE, IN BOOKS, IN HIS DREAMS.
HE IS A BORN ADVENTURER.
THOUGH HE HASN'T TRAVELED
MUCH BEYOND BROOKLYN IN REAL
LIFE, HIS IMAGINATION HAS AL-
READY TAKEN HIM AROUND THE
WORLD.

ALEX FERNANDEZ

GW: HELLO, ALEX.

ALEX: Ghostwriter! *¡Buenos días! ¿Qué tal?*

GW: WHAT?

ALEX: Just throwing a little Spanish at you. I said "Hello. What's up?"

GW: SO *"BUENOS DÍAS"* MEANS "HELLO"?

ALEX: *Sí,* more or less. Literally it means "good day." But that's the same as saying hello.

GW: I CAN SEE BY READING THE BOXES AND THE PACKAGES AROUND YOU THAT YOU'RE IN YOUR FAMILY'S GROCERY STORE. ARE YOU BUSY?

ALEX: Not anymore. When I first came in, I swept the floor. Then I helped my father restock the shelves. Then Papa had to pick up some *cebollas* and stuff from the farmers' market, so I'm watching the *bodega* until he gets back.

GW: *CEBOLLAS? BODEGA?*

ALEX: *Cebollas* is Spanish for "onions." A *bodega* is a store.

GW: IT MUST BE FUN TO SPEAK SPANISH.

ALEX: Fun? I don't even think about it. Speaking Spanish is just normal to me. I mean, a kid who speaks English doesn't wake up every morning thinking about how much fun it is to speak English, does he?

GW: I DOUBT IT.

ALEX: Well, it's the same with me. My mother and father speak Spanish around the house, so I speak Spanish, too. It's no big deal.

GW: WHERE ARE YOUR PARENTS FROM?

ALEX: El Salvador. That's a tiny country in Central America. A civil war was going on there, so my father and mother left El Salvador before I was born. They've never gone back, either. But I'm going to visit El Salvador someday. And I'm going to climb the Izalco volcano, just like my father did. Yes, I'll become a great explorer! I will laugh in the face of danger!

GW: MY GOODNESS! PLEASE BE CAREFUL.

ALEX: Where would we be if people were afraid

to take chances? Think about this: If my parents weren't willing to take chances, I might not be here today.

GW: HOW IS THAT?

ALEX: My parents took a chance just coming to the United States. First they had to sneak *out* of El Salvador, then they had to sneak *into* the States.

GW: THE UNITED STATES DIDN'T WANT YOUR PARENTS TO COME?

ALEX: See, usually when people from another country come to live here, they have to get the government's permission. They have to fill out a lot of forms and stuff. My parents didn't have time to complete the proper papers. They had to get out of El Salvador fast because my father's life was in danger. My father didn't like the El Salvadoran government, and he spoke out about it. So the government didn't like *him*.

GW: WHAT DID YOUR PARENTS DO?

ALEX: They snuck out of El Salvador. They traveled north for many days and nights, through Guatemala and Mexico, until they reached the Texas border. Sometimes they had to lie down in cold, dark ditches and hide. And sometimes they had to crawl under fences and through small spaces so that they would not be seen. This was especially hard for my mother because she was pregnant—with me.

GW: WHAT WOULD HAVE HAPPENED IF SOMEONE HAD SEEN THEM?

ALEX: They could have been sent back to El Salvador. And, believe me, that government wasn't nice to people who tried to escape. But my parents made it across the Texas border, and some kind people were waiting there to help them out. The best part of the story is that soon after my parents arrived in Texas, I was born. I'm a Texan by birth. So I'm an American.

GW: IF YOU'RE AMERICAN, THEN YOUR PARENTS ARE AMERICAN, TOO, AREN'T THEY?

ALEX: No, it doesn't work that way. In order for my parents to become citizens, they'd have to apply for citizenship. That means they'd have to go through a long legal process. They haven't done that yet. I don't think Papa wants to.

GW: ARE THEY IN DANGER OF BEING SENT BACK TO EL SALVADOR?

ALEX: No way! They've got amnesty from the U.S. government. That means the government says it's okay for them to stay here. They're cool.

GW: THAT'S GOOD!

ALEX: Since I'm an American, I can do a lot of things that my parents can't. For example, I could become president of the United States. I'd like that! True, I lost when I ran for school president a while back, but you can't win 'em all. This is a great country, but there are a lot of things about it I'd like to see fixed. I think I'd be a good president, if I say so myself.

GW: PRESIDENT FERNANDEZ.

ALEX: It has a nice ring to it, doesn't it?

GW: IT DOES.

ALEX: And when I become president, I'll make sure that the people of the United States know about the concerns of people in other parts of the world, too. My pen pals could help me get their messages across.

GW: DO YOU HAVE A LOT OF PEN PALS?

ALEX: A zillion. They're all over the world, too—Brazil, Switzerland, Germany, Kenya, France, you name it. It's great talking to them about how their lives are different from mine. When I get older, I'm going to visit every one of them. I'll ride a raft down the Amazon River with Lucia in Brazil. In Switzerland, I'll climb the Alps with Heidi. In Germany, Steffi and I will visit the place where the Berlin Wall was. And in Kenya, Nana has promised to take me on safari.

GW: WHAT ABOUT IN PARIS?

ALEX: Well, that's up to Gigi. She likes to walk along the banks of the Seine and visit the Louvre.

GW: THE LOUVRE?

ALEX: It's some famous art museum they have there. Personally, I could probably live without seeing it, but Gigi likes that kind of stuff.

GW: I SEE.

ALEX: Now, don't get any fancy ideas, Ghost-writer. Gigi and I are just friends.

GW: I SEE.

ALEX: When I get older, Gigi and I are going to open a detective agency together.

GW: I THOUGHT THAT WHEN YOU GOT OLDER, YOU WERE GOING TO CLIMB THE VOLCANO OF EL SALVADOR.

ALEX: I will.

GW: AND VISIT YOUR PEN PALS IN BRA-
ZIL, SWITZERLAND, KENYA, GERMANY,
AND FRANCE.

ALEX: For sure!

GW: AND AREN'T YOU GOING TO BE-
COME PRESIDENT?

ALEX: If I'm lucky.

GW: BUT IF YOU DO ALL THOSE THINGS,
WHEN WILL YOU HAVE TIME TO OPEN
UP A DETECTIVE AGENCY? YOU'LL BE
TOO BUSY!

ALEX: I'll find the time. You know, there was this
slogan that the New York Mets used back in
1973. Back then they were a pretty bad baseball
team. Midway through the season they were in
last place. No one even *thought* about them making it to the World Series, which is where the two
top teams play each other to see who's best. People
dissed the Mets, big time.

GW: DISSED?

ALEX: You know, disrespected. No one thought
they had a prayer. But Tug McGraw, a pitcher for
the Mets, came up with this slogan. He said: "You
gotta believe." And pretty soon everyone started

believing. The Mets went from worst to first in their division. And they made it to the World Series after all!

GW: YOU GOTTA BELIEVE. I UNDERSTAND.

ALEX: Somehow I'll do it all—you'll see, Ghostwriter. Oops, here comes Papa. I'd better go help him with the onions. *Hasta luego, mi amigo.* That means see you later, friend.

DAVID LOPEZ

If you visit David Lopez's bedroom at his home in New Jersey, you'll see a bed, a desk with a computer on it, a ceiling fan, and posters of the Chicago Bulls and the New York Mets hanging on his wall. But here's some advice: Don't look at David's wall too closely.

"There are a lot of holes in my wall right now," David says with a laugh. David, who plays Alex on *Ghostwriter*, also has a dart board in his room. Sometimes he misses the target.

But that's okay because David doesn't miss out on too many other things. "David is an all-American athlete," says Sheldon Turnipseed, who plays Jamal on the show. He and David have become good friends since *Ghostwriter* began. "He plays football, basketball, baseball—you name it, he plays it."

"I love running, I love playing sports," says David. "I'm glad people invented sports."

Before *Ghostwriter* began, David was on a "traveling" baseball team. His team would play other teams from nearby towns. Sometimes David pitched, but he liked playing catcher better. Why? A catcher gets to throw runners out at second base. "Yeah," says David. "That's fun."

But it's a different kind of fun than skiing. David skied for the first time in 1991. He went with a friend and his friend's family to Lake Placid, which is in New York. In 1980 the Winter Olympics were held there. Some of the mountains around Lake Placid are very tall and very steep.

David and his friend were on vacation for seven days. During the first few days David skied down the "bunny" slope. This is a little slope, or hill, that beginners use. David fell a lot, but he liked skiing. And he got better at it. By his last day of vacation, he had worked his way up to the highest ski trail there was. Although he was scared when he looked down the mountain, David was also surprised by what he found.

"It was quiet, still—and it was actually warm

up there," he remembers. "All you could see was a light little fog. Nothing moved; it was, like, no breeze up there. It was just so beautiful."

David's heart was racing as he began skiing down the mountain, but he made it. What an adventure!

Back home in New Jersey, though, David's life is pretty normal. He lives with his mother, Veronica, father, Oscar, older sister, Windy, and pet parakeet, Willie the Third, in one part of a large two-family house. Four of David's aunts live in the other part.

David knew from the time he was very young that he wanted to act. He told his mother that he'd like to be the next James Bond. They still joke about that. When David was nine years old he started taking acting lessons. "At first I used to get very nervous. A lot. But after a while it was okay."

Although David likes acting, he doesn't like to watch himself on TV. The only reason he even saw the first episode of *Ghostwriter* is because he was at Sheldon's house and Sheldon made him watch it. Whenever he looks at himself, David sees a million things wrong. "My feet are kind of big," he says. "And I'm too skinny; I want to gain a little weight. And my hair is so dark—but that's all right, I guess. And my teeth. Even though I had braces, there's something wrong with my teeth. I don't know what it is. Every time I look, I wish I could just take them out and get a nice pair."

David doesn't have a girlfriend right now, but he knows what he likes in a girl. "I like them when they're funny, and when they're not over-protective," he says. "When they're just overall nice. I like a sweet girl."

He also likes *Young Indiana Jones* and *The Best of National Geographic.* They're two of his favorite television shows. "I'm really interested in the world," he says. "I like to know what's going on, what's out there. Someday I want to go to Australia and see the Great Barrier Reef. That would be nice."

Someday David would also like to race cars for a living. "I've seen a lot of crashes," he says, "but I still want to race."

Yes, David *really* loves adventures. And he loves

to travel. One of his biggest adventures came when he traveled to Colombia, a country in South America. Many of David's relatives live there. David has visited Colombia a few times over the years, but a trip that he took when he was about four years old really stands out in his mind.

The excitement began even before David and his family reached their final destination, a tiny island off Colombia. The only way to get there is by canoe!

The water was very rough as they passed through a place called Punta Tiburón, which means Shark's Point. If the boat had capsized or turned over, the sharks might have been happy—but David's family would have been in big trouble! Fortunately, the group made it to the island safe and sound.

Once they got to the tiny jungle island, David's sister, Windy, got sick and had to be taken to the island nurse. The infirmary was just a room with medical instruments and a bed in it. Finally Windy was treated and they all went to their island "home." It turned out to be a hut made of sticks, with no toilet and no electricity. All around were three-inch flying cockroaches. What a welcome! In these strange surroundings David and his family went to sleep.

When they woke up the next morning, rain puddles were in their beds. That was the good news! "The bad news was, a monkey had gone to the bathroom on my aunt's head," says David. "She woke up screaming."

The adventures continued. David and his family went to the other side of the island, where a river ran near the ocean. Huge waves crashed down on them while they were in the river. Although David was holding his mother's hand when a wave hit, somehow he was swept away. He was thrown to the bottom of the river. He was drowning!

"Then this kid jumped in and saved me," says David. "If it wasn't for that kid, I wouldn't be here right now."

It's a good thing he is. *Ghostwriter* wouldn't be the same without him!

SOMETIMES BIG THINGS COME IN SMALL PACKAGES. IF YOU NEED PROOF, JUST LOOK AT GABY FERNANDEZ.

ALTHOUGH GABY IS THE YOUNGEST MEMBER OF THE TEAM, THAT DOESN'T HOLD HER BACK. FAR FROM IT! GABY KNOWS A MILLION DIFFERENT THINGS ABOUT A MILLION DIFFERENT SUBJECTS. SHE IS CURIOUS ABOUT *EVERYTHING*. AT TIMES, TALKING TO HER CAN BE CONFUSING. BUT IT'S ALWAYS FUN.

HAVE YOU EVER STEPPED INSIDE A HUMAN WHIRLWIND? IF NOT, HOLD ON TIGHT. HERE WE GO!

•••••••••••••••••••••••••••••••••

GABY FERNANDEZ

•••••••••••••••••••••••••••••••••

GW: GREETINGS, GABY.

GABY: Ghostwriter, you'll never guess what I found out today. I'm famous! Actually, I'm not really famous, but my name is. That's almost the same thing, right?

GW: WELL . . .

GABY: My father says he named me after this lady named Gabriela Mistral, who was a famous poet in Chile. Papa likes her poetry a lot. I'm just glad he doesn't like taxis a lot, too. Then my name might be Gaby *Cabbie* Fernandez. Imagine living with a name like that! I'd never tell people, of course. I'd go by my initials: G. C. Fernandez. Pretty cool, right? Like L. L. Cool J.

GW: TAXIS?

GABY: You need to have a middle name for the initials to work. I mean, G. Fernandez just doesn't cut it. And—wouldn't you know it—I don't even *have* a middle name. But that's okay because one day I'm going to choose one. It will be perfect. What do you think of Angelina? Gabriela Angelina Fernandez. And María's all right. But not Consuela—definitely not Consuela. My mother's friend, Doña Consuela, used to pinch me on the cheek every time she saw me. I didn't appreciate that at all. I think people who do that must really not like kids. Anyway, the name Consuela is out.

GW: HOW ABOUT "WHIRLWIND"?

GABY: *Whirlwind?* What kind of name is that? Ghostwriter, sometimes I don't understand you! But the word *whirlwind* sounds a little like Corwin, doesn't it? Mr. Corwin was my math teacher last year. Did I ever tell you about what happened between me and Mr. Corwin? Oh, you'll love this! See . . . we're in class and for some reason Mr. Corwin starts talking about birthdays. Fine. He says that he was born in 1956. And I say—very, very quietly, I might add—that when he was born, he must have really made a monkey out of himself. Monkey—get it? Unfortunately, Mr. Corwin didn't think it was funny. Where's his sense of humor?

GW: MAYBE YOU HURT HIS FEELINGS.

GABY: Oh, Ghostwriter, Mr. Corwin said he was born in 1956. Don't you see? In the Chinese calendar 1956 was the year of the monkey. Everybody knows that!

GW: I DIDN'T.

GABY: Well, now you do. Anyway, you probably did know it—you just don't remember, like you don't remember much about your past. But Mr. Corwin's a *teacher*! You know, Tina and I were thinking about making a video about teachers. We were going to ask them all sorts of questions. Where were you born? Who was your favorite teacher? Why do you like teaching? Stuff like that. Then we were going to show the video to our classmates. Well, if we *do* make that video, I'll ask Mr. Corwin if his favorite pet is the monkey. Then I'll run!

GW: VERY INTERESTING.

GABY: Uh-huh. You know what? Once Tina and I signed the school video camera out for a weekend and I took secret pictures of Alex. It was great! I felt like a spy or something. Oh, Ghostwriter, if only you could see more than just words!

See, I got up before Alex and hid the video camera in the shades, aimed at his bed. Then I just sat there very quietly. Alex finally woke up. He kind of stretched and yawned and lay there, and I thought that this tape was going to be kind of boring, when all of a sudden he jumps out of the bed and starts singing "I'm Bad." That's an old Michael Jackson song. Did you know that Michael Jackson started singing when he was even younger than I am? He did. Anyway, I guess that Alex thought he was alone, so he didn't feel funny about singing and dancing around in his pajamas. That's the best part! He was wearing these faded old Spider-Man™ pajamas that Tía Rosa gave him a few birthdays ago. And he was dancing around singing "I'm Bad!" It was so funny, I almost laughed out loud.

GW: SO YOU GOT HIS WHOLE PERFORMANCE ON VIDEOTAPE?

GABY: Yup, and I still have the tape. Alex should treat me *very* nicely in the future or else . . .

GW: OR ELSE YOU MIGHT SHOW THE TAPE TO SOMEONE ELSE?

GABY: Well, I'd never *really* show the tape to

anyone else—but Alex doesn't have to know that.

GW: I SEE.

GABY: I mean, Alex sometimes bothers me, but I guess as brothers go he's cool. Did I ever tell you how he stuck up for me the time that jerk Terrence Dillard "borrowed" my bicycle and refused to give it back? Hey, did you know that the most famous bicycle race in the world is over two thousand miles long and lasts more than twenty days? It's called the Tour de France and it's held in France every year. More than two thousand miles—wow! Imagine the kind of shape you have to be in to compete in that! Once I tried jogging two miles with my friend Lisa, but I don't think I made it two blocks. I really need to work on my stamina. Maybe I should try out for the track team.

GW: YOU WERE TALKING ABOUT TERRENCE DILLARD.

GABY: Right. He borrowed my bicycle, and every time I told him I wanted it back, he told me I'd have to take it from him. Naturally, I couldn't catch him. I mean, he was on my bike and all. He must have played with me like that for an hour!

GW: HE SOUNDS LIKE A BULLY.

GABY: He was. And he was a lot bigger than me, too. I didn't tell Alex what was going on because I was ashamed, but Alex heard about it anyway from some of the other kids. Boy, was he mad. He came running down the street and he caught up to that creepy Terrence Dillard, bike and all. He made Terrence get off the bike and told him that if he wanted a bike so badly, he'd better go out and buy one of his own.

GW: AND WHAT DID TERRENCE DO?

GABY: He was really scared. He gave me my bike back. And he never messed with me again, either. And do you know what Alex did? He told me that if anyone ever messed with me again like that, he wanted to know about it. And then he walked away—kind of like in those old cowboy pictures where the good guy rides off into the sunset. It was great!

Hey, I better go; my stomach is growling and if I remember correctly, there should be some chocolate cake left in the kitchen. Talk to you later?

GW: I'M HERE WHENEVER YOU NEED ME. ENJOY THE CAKE, GABY. GOOD-BYE!

MAYTEANA MORALES

When you look up the word *gabby* in the dictionary, you'll see that it means "talkative." But Mayteana Morales, the actress who plays Gaby Fernandez on *Ghostwriter,* is *not* talkative. In fact, she seems very shy. At least at first.

After a while, though, Mayteana opens up. And once she really gets rolling, watch out! One minute Mayteana and Blaze Berdahl (Lenni) are singing an En Vogue tune on the *Ghostwriter* set. The next minute they're working on a dance step. Then later Mayteana is playing catch with a member of the crew. She sure has a lot of energy! It's easy to understand why her nickname is "Mighty Mouse." Mayteana is always in motion!

"I like to play tag, kickball, and basketball," she says. "And I love to dance. I take two classes every Saturday, ballet and jazz." Mayteana stopped taking a lot of other classes, though, when she got her role on *Ghostwriter*. Tap dancing, acting, singing, modern dance—all those classes came to an end. At least for a while. "I still want to take them, but I just don't have any time."

You see, although Mayteana says that it's lots of fun working on *Ghostwriter,* it's still a job. And like Sheldon (Jamal), Blaze (Lenni), and the other young actors in the cast, Mayteana is supposed to be in school. The solution? Everyone on the show goes to school *at* work.

Usually the actors arrive at the studio by 8 in the morning. From 8 A.M. until 10 A.M. they do schoolwork. Tutors (private teachers) sit in a small room with Mayteana and the other actors and work with them on different subjects. Then, from 10 A.M. until around 6 P.M., the kids tape the show. Sometimes taping is over before 6; sometimes it goes on much later than that. When an actor isn't in a particular scene, he or she will often go back to the "classroom" to be tutored. The rules say that these young actors must spend at least three hours a day in school. Without blackboards, recess, and lots of other classmates, though, the "school" on the *Ghostwriter* set is certainly different from other schools!

So, does Mayteana miss her friends back at her regular school in Hempstead, New York? "Not really," she says. "I feel okay because I know I'm going to see them again. I like tutoring. But one thing I do miss about school is playing double dutch."

Mayteana's favorite subject in school is spelling. She's okay in math and she likes history a lot. "Yeah, history is pretty cool, but sometimes I don't get it," she says. "Then I have to read the whole chapter over."

No problem. Reading is one of Mayteana's favorite things to do. She is very particular about what she reads. "I don't like those 'teenager' books," Mayteana says. "Mostly I like classics. I really liked *Of Mice and Men* by John Steinbeck. At the end there was a problem you couldn't solve. In all those teenager books they always find solutions. That's not real."

Yet Mayteana likes to read fantasies, too. Another favorite of hers is *Alice's Adventures in Won-*

derland. "I liked the way they talked—they used all these words that sometimes I couldn't understand," she says.

If she has a problem understanding something, Mayteana can just turn to her parents for help. And when she's at her regular school, she doesn't have to turn very far, either. Mayteana's dad, Xavier Morales, is a bilingual teacher. He helps Spanish-speaking students learn English. And he teaches at Mayteana's school! When she's not working on *Ghostwriter,* Mayteana often sees Mr. Morales during the day.

"He always used to bother me," says Mayteana. "Sometimes he'd want to talk to me about chorus or tell me that I'd have to practice for a spelling bee. But it was good having him in the school . . . sometimes. Sometimes it was bad."

Mayteana's mother, Miladys, also worked in a school, but at a different one. Mrs. Morales was a school nurse and a teacher. Lately, though, Mrs. Morales has been helping with Mayteana's career. She has been taking her daughter to auditions and acting as her agent.

Mr. Morales was born in Puerto Rico and Mrs.

Morales was born in El Salvador. Is it any surprise, then, that like David Lopez (Alex), Mayteana speaks Spanish?

In fact, Mayteana's name is a tribute to her family. Her mother's mother, María Ester Cordero, was nicknamed Mayte. Her father's mother is Ana Morales. When Mayteana was born, Miladys Morales combined her mother's name with her mother-in-law's name. The result was Mayteana.

Just as Gaby is the youngest member of the *Ghostwriter* team, Mayteana is the youngest member of her family. But Mayteana is *much* younger than everyone else in her family. One of her brothers, Angel, is in the marines. He's stationed in Virginia. Another brother, Alberto, works as an assistant teacher and goes to college. Mayteana's sister, Jennifer, is also in college. Both Alberto and Jennifer live at home with Mayteana, their mom, and a grandmother. Sometimes a great-aunt lives with them, too. At times it's a very crowded household. But there's always someone to talk to.

When Mayteana has some time off, she likes to go ice skating or roller skating with her friends. In the summertime she likes to swim in the pool

Sheldon gets his off-screen kicks studying karate.

What, you want me to do that scene again?

Mighty Mouse
Mayteana Morales in
a mischievous
moment.

PARTY!!

Avid reader, singer, dancer, and actress, Blaze Berdahl wears many hats.

Arthur A. Murphy

Who says work can't be comical?

Arthur A. Murphy

David tips his hat to Todd after another great performance.

Arthur A. Murphy

Move over, En Vogue! Here come the
Ghostwriter Girls.

Oh, the glamour of working on TV—NOT!

A "peaceful" moment off camera.

Arthur A. Murphy

Blaze and Tram-Anh watch their friends on camera.

Arthur A. Murphy

Spike Lee does the "write" thing, pictured here hangin' with the Ghostwriter team.

Arthur A. Murphy

Arthur A. Murphy

Sometimes the kids on the team have more energy than the grown-ups!

Arthur A. Murphy

Smile,
you're on
camera!

Seth Greenberg

in her backyard. She used to enjoy playing basketball in her driveway, but her family had to take
the hoop down. Too many strangers were stop-
ping by the Morales house to play ball. "I felt bad
because that ruined my time to play," says Mayteana. "But we weren't going to take the hoop
down and put it up every time I wanted to play.
That gets tiring."

Is it possible that Mighty Mouse could get
tired? Not!

Mayteana's favorite color is black, some of her
favorite singers are Vanessa Williams and Boyz II
Men, and actors she admires include Dustin Hoff-
man and Jodie Foster. One of her hobbies is collecting trolls. That hobby began when she and a
friend bought troll pins. Mayteana's had hot-pink
hair, a jewel in its stomach, and a surprised look
on its face. "He was so cute!" Mayteana says. Now
she has at least twelve trolls in her collection, including one treasured troll pencil.

Mayteana began acting when she was about
four years old. Her first job was doing a Coca-Cola
commercial. In it she danced with two other actors
who were supposed to be her grandparents. May-

teana didn't say anything in that commercial, but she had fun. She began taking acting classes when she was six. "I liked acting classes. We'd do improvisations and games to learn how to act."

Eventually Mayteana got more acting jobs. Some of the movies she appeared in were *New Jack City, The Prince of Tides,* and *Mo' Better Blues.* Mayteana also had small roles on the television shows *Where in the World Is Carmen Sandiego?* and *The Cosby Show.*

"Bill Cosby was funny," Mayteana says. "He was making all these faces. And the girl who played Olivia—Raven—we played games with her. She was cute!"

Of course, Mayteana's biggest role is the one she now has on *Ghostwriter.* And it's her favorite role, too. But she really has to use her acting skills to play her part. Why? She and Gaby aren't very much alike, Mayteana admits. "Gaby's nosy, she talks a lot, and she has this big brother who kind of hates her guts."

But there is one thing that Mayteana has in common with her character: Gaby is smart. Mayteana laughs. "Well, I am, too," she says.

And do you know what? Mighty Mouse is right!

TINA NGUYEN IS AT HER BEST WHEN SHE'S BEHIND THE VIDEO CAMERA. SHE MAY SOMETIMES SEEM QUIET NEXT TO HER FRIEND GABY, BUT HER VIDEOS ARE *LOUD* WITH AC- TION. THOUGH I CAN'T ACTUALLY SEE THEM, TINA KEEPS ME UP-TO- DATE BY WRITING EVERYTHING DOWN IN HER VIDEO LOGBOOK. I LIKE HER STORIES!

TINA NGUYEN

GW: HELLO, TINA.

TINA: Ghostwriter! I was just about to start my homework. I have to do some math before I go help my parents in the tailor shop.

GW: WHAT DO YOU DO TO HELP?

TINA: Mostly I wait on customers who come in to have their clothes mended or altered. I don't do the sewing. I'm not good enough. My mother does some of it, but my father does the really delicate stuff.

GW: DO YOU ENJOY WORKING IN THE SHOP?

TINA: "Sew" far, "sew" good. Get it?

GW: HA, HA. YOU REALLY KEEP ME IN STITCHES.

TINA: Hey, that's funny!

GW: HOW DID YOUR FATHER BECOME SO SKILLED AS A TAILOR?

TINA: Well, he's been doing it for more than twenty years. He worked as a tailor back in Vietnam, too.

GW: LENNI TOLD ME SOMETHING ABOUT VIETNAM. SHE SAID THERE WAS A WAR THERE. DO YOU KNOW ABOUT IT?

TINA: Sure. Remember, my family is from Vietnam. And even though I was born in the United States, I've taken courses on Vietnamese history at the community center. We meet on Saturday mornings. I've also learned to read and write Vietnamese—that's fun! So what do you want to know about the war?

GW: DID A LOT OF PEOPLE GET HURT?

TINA: Yeah, lots. The war changed everybody's life there. Take my family, for instance. My father and mother lived in Saigon, the capital of South Vietnam—that's the part of the country that lost the war. When the war was over, things got so bad in Saigon that they decided to leave. But they couldn't just go. They had to sneak out of Vietnam because the government didn't want people to leave.

GW: ALEX AND GABY'S PARENTS HAD TO SNEAK OUT OF THEIR COUNTRY, TOO!

TINA: Really? Well, my father and my mother and my brother, Tuan, got on a fishing boat late one night. Lots of other people who wanted to escape were on the boat, too. Their boat sailed for four days before reaching Thailand—that's a country near Vietnam. It was a very dangerous journey. And once they arrived in Thailand, the people there wanted them to leave. Vietnamese were not welcome. But in the end it all worked out. My uncle Liam helped my parents come to the United States and get settled in their own tailor shop in New York City. My little sister, Linda, and I were born here—in America.

GW: DO YOUR PARENTS WANT TO GO BACK TO VIETNAM?

TINA: They don't talk about it, at least not with me. But they definitely want us to live the Vietnamese way.

GW: WHAT IS THE VIETNAMESE WAY?

TINA: We eat Vietnamese food, and we celebrate the Vietnamese holidays, and stuff like that. And I guess Vietnamese kids are taught to behave in a certain way toward our parents. Like, I could never be as casual with my parents as Lenni is with her dad.

GW: DO YOU LIKE THE VIETNAMESE WAY?

TINA: I guess. There's a lot I love about it. The food, the music. But sometimes it's hard to explain to my friends why I do things differently from them.

My brother, Tuan, hates it. All he wants is to be American. He's really a pain about it.

GW: HOW?

TINA: Well, it seems like he doesn't respect my father at all. They're always getting into huge arguments. It's kind of scary, Ghostwriter. They get so angry! I'm afraid that one day Tuan will just leave home and never come back. Or maybe my father will throw him out. Either way, it would be awful.

GW: WHAT DO THEY ARGUE ABOUT?

TINA: Oh, dumb stuff. My father thinks Tuan's hair is too long, and that Tuan is lazy and plays his music too loud. Tuan's in a rock band, you know. And Tuan thinks that my father is too strict and old-fashioned and expects too much from him. I don't know—I guess lots of fathers and sons argue about stuff like this. I just wish it didn't have to happen in my home.

GW: MAYBE THINGS WILL GET BETTER.

TINA: Yeah . . . someday. In the future my father and brother will probably look back on these days and laugh. I might even make a film about it: *The Trouble with Tuan*. Hey, how's that for a title?

GW: CATCHY! TINA, PLEASE EXPLAIN HOW FILMS WORK.

TINA: Okay, I'll try. You know that photographs are still pictures, right?

GW: RIGHT.

TINA: Well, films are moving pictures. That is, they're a whole bunch of still pictures put together in a row. When you look at each of them really quickly, it seems as though they're all the same picture—only they're moving.

GW: DON'T YOUR HANDS GET TIRED FROM MOVING THE PICTURES SO FAST?

TINA: No, you don't make the pictures move with your hands, Ghostwriter! Video and film cameras use special film. A video or film camera can take dozens of pictures in a second. Each one of these shots is called a frame. Thousands and thousands of frames make one film. And the camera does most of the work.

GW: I WISH I COULD SEE A FILM.

TINA: I wish you could, too. You'd love *Casablanca*. The best scene of all comes at the end, when Humphrey Bogart is saying good-bye to Ingrid Bergman. See, they're really incredibly in love with each other, but they can't be together because she's married to someone else. It's so romantic! They're standing in all this swirling fog, and Ingrid's crying, and Bogie says to her, "Here's looking at you, kid." And then he kind of smiles at her and that's that. Good-bye forever.

GW: WHEN YOU TELL IT I CAN ALMOST SEE IT MYSELF.

TINA: Someday I'm going to make a film like that.

GW: I WOULDN'T BE AT ALL SURPRISED.

TINA: Oh, no—look at the time! I'm never going to make any films at all if I don't get my homework done *now*! Sorry, Ghostwriter, I've got to go. Talk to you soon!

TRAM-ANH TRAN

Not too many things seem to bother Tram-anh Tran (Tina). Tram-anh (she likes to be called "Tremaine") is the kind of person who finds something good in almost everything. She rarely talks about the bad. But when asked she admits that, sometimes, people get on her nerves. Particularly boy people.

"They fool around in class," she says. "And then they just come up to you and hit you for no good reason or trip you. That's very annoying."

But even boys have their good points—especially some of her classmates at St. John Chrysostom School in Chester, Pennsylvania. "They're really nice," she says. "The people in my class, we've known each other since, like, first grade. They're all very caring."

Tram-anh is popular and very active in her school. In the seventh grade she was elected secretary of the student council. She's not in the student government this year, but perhaps that's just as well. Since getting a job on *Ghostwriter*, Tram-anh can't go to school much anymore. In fact, she can't even go home much anymore, either. Since her home is about 120 miles from New York City, where *Ghostwriter* is filmed, Tram-anh lives with an uncle near the city during the week. She doesn't get to go home until the weekends. And then she has lots of catching up to do.

First there are piano lessons. Tram-anh has taken lessons since she was five years old. Sometimes she performs in festivals or recitals. She'll memorize a song or two and play it in front of an audience. Other young pianists will also perform. Then ribbons are handed out to those who did best.

Tram-anh has gotten many ribbons for her piano playing, but she may have a tougher time getting them in the future. The uncle that she stays with during the week doesn't have a piano, so Tram-anh can't really practice until she goes home on the weekends. "It's hard, but I practice a lot when I'm home," she says. Often she spends an hour and a half a day practicing.

But the piano isn't Tram-anh's only hobby. "I don't watch TV a lot, and whenever I'm not practicing the piano or cleaning up or helping my mom or dad, I'm practicing gymnastics." Gymnastics has been a passion of Tram-anh's for a long time. She particularly liked seeing tapes of Nadia Comaneci, a Romanian gymnast who won three gold medals in the 1976 Olympics. "She's an old gymnast," says Tram-anh, "but she was really good." So a few years ago when her parents gave her the choice of studying ballet or joining a gymnastics club, Tram-anh quickly knew what she wanted to do.

Tram-anh's specialty in gymnastics is the vault. "I'm a fast runner, and if you're really fast that helps you a lot," she says. Before *Ghostwriter* she used to take two or three gymnastics classes a week. Now she competes with her club when she can. But she still practices: She'll often go to her attic during the weekend to work on dance routines, strengthen her arms and legs, or do cartwheels. Although she'd like to be a great gymnast, she really doesn't dream of trying out for the Olympic team. "You'd have to work out every single day to get that good," she says. "I don't know about that."

She'd like to be an actress when she grows up. But since show business is so crazy, she wants to have something to fall back on. Tram-anh's plan is to go to college and study law. Then, if acting doesn't work out, she can always make a living as a lawyer.

Just like Tina's parents, Tram-anh's parents were born in Vietnam. Her father, Phiet, is now a senior engineer for a company that makes airplanes. Her mother, Lien, used to work as a pharmacy technician; now she spends most of her time escorting Tram-anh to her lessons and acting jobs.

Tram-anh was born in Thailand, but she and her parents moved to America when she was about six months old. Tram-anh has two younger sisters, Uyen-Ly and Hanh-Tien (who plays Tina's sister on *Ghostwriter*). Although Tram-anh gets along with both of them, she sometimes wishes that things had been different. "I wish I had an older brother," she says. "I think it would be fun to have someone sticking up for you instead of you sticking up for someone."

Since Tram-anh is only a year older than Uyen-Ly, they're pretty close. They sometimes share books and clothes., They even share a hobby. Uyen-Ly taught Tram-anh how to make Guatemalan friendship dolls. These are small dolls, no more than two inches high, which are made out of toothpicks. "We glue the toothpicks together or we use wire and wrap it with floss," says Tram-anh. "It takes me two days to make one, but my sister can make one in fifteen minutes."

Basically Tram-anh is a homebody. She doesn't hang out much, but when she does it's usually with her four best buddies from school. "We go to the movies or just hang out at each other's houses," says Tram-anh. "Whenever one of us gets in trouble, the others help. It's like a sister-group thing."

But about the only time Tram-anh gets in trouble—at least with her parents—is when she hits one of her *real* sisters. Otherwise, she says, she's a pretty good kid. She knows that her parents expect her to treat them with respect, so she does.

"My parents were raised Vietnamese, so I'm raised Vietnamese," Tram-anh observes. "I can't just yell back at them. I'd get in bad trouble if I ever did. I haven't tried it yet. And I'm not going to!"

Tram-anh *has* tried cooking, though, and she's good at it. If you were to visit her home, she might fix some of her favorites: rice, crab soup, a stir-fried dish (like vegetables with meat or shrimp), and fried fish with a special sauce. "I make lots of Vietnamese dishes," she says. "Sometimes I cook for my parents."

It was Mr. and Mrs. Tran who first got Tram-anh interested in show business. They entered her in a talent contest when she was about six years old. For her talent segment Tram-anh sang a song. She won! One of the judges in the contest was so impressed with her that he offered to become her manager. He is still her manager today.

Over the years Tram-anh has done commercials and television shows for local stations. But none of her previous projects were as big as *Ghostwriter*. She says that the best thing about being on the show is meeting so many new people. And the worst thing? "The long hours. Definitely the long hours."

If only there were 48 hours in a day, 336 hours in a week! Then Tram-anh might have time to do all the things she can't do now. She'd practice gymnastics and the piano every day and find some really great horror books to read. She'd paint her room white with black splotches all over (black is her favorite color) and listen to loud music on her radio. She'd travel to Vietnam to visit some relatives and to Walt Disney World to ride on Big Thunder Mountain again. And she'd take ice-skating lessons. "I've heard lots of people say it's fun, but I've never really tried it," Tram-anh says. "So I'd like to try that."

But for now those things must wait. Ever since a friendly ghost entered Tram-anh's life, nothing is as it used to be. Sometimes even Tram-anh can't believe the way her life is turning out. "It's so surprising! I never thought I'd be an actress," she says. Then she smiles. "But I'm glad it happened to me."

THE NEWEST MEMBER OF THE TEAM
IS A POET. HIS NAME IS ROB BAKER,
AND HE LIVES IN A WORLD OF MAG-
ICAL WORDS. SOMETIMES IT SEEMS
HARD FOR HIM TO LEAVE HIS PRI-
VATE WORLD AND BE WITH PEOPLE.
WHEN HE DOES, THOUGH, HE IS A
RARE FRIEND.

ROB BAKER

GW: HELLO, ROB.

ROB: Hey, Ghostwriter. I'm just finishing up a new poem.

GW: MAY I READ IT?

ROB: Uh . . . maybe another time. No offense, but it's kind of private.

Can I ask you something? Do you ever get lonely, Ghostwriter?

GW: SOMETIMES. NOT SO OFTEN, NOW THAT I HAVE YOU AND THE REST OF THE TEAM TO TALK TO.

ROB: That's cool. You know, I like talking to you, too. And the team. It's kind of neat being part of the team. I think.

GW: MAYBE YOU'RE STILL GETTING USED TO IT.

ROB: Yeah, that's exactly right. Hey, guess what? I just got a letter from my brother, Jason.

GW: HOW IS HE?

ROB: Good. The last time he wrote to me, he said he might become a vegetarian—you know, someone who doesn't eat meat. There's this huge garden at his school where the students grow cabbage, corn, tomatoes, and a whole bunch of other vegetables. Jason is really into it. He read this great book that talks about why eating meat is bad for you, and he said he'll give it to me the next time he comes home for a visit.

GW: WHEN WILL THAT BE?

ROB: Soon, I hope. The Museum of Natural History has this slammin' exhibit on cars from the 1930s through the 1960s, but it ends in two months. Jason would get a kick out of that! He just got his driver's license, you know.

GW: IS THAT GOOD?

ROB: Yes. It means Jason can legally drive a car now. It's excellent. Especially after the driving instructor Jason had—what a jerk!

GW: WHAT DO YOU MEAN?

ROB: Jason's instructor was one of those people

who think that if someone can't hear, they must be stupid. I mean, Jason's deaf, but he's certainly not dumb. Yet the instructor kept yelling at him, as if that made a difference. I mean, the guy could have shouted all day long and Jason still wouldn't have been able to hear what he said. But he can understand what you're saying as long as he can read your lips. Sheesh! Some people just don't get it!

GW: PEOPLE CAN BE THOUGHTLESS.

ROB: Yeah. If only hearing people could just remember that people who are deaf are the same as everyone else. They just can't hear.

You know what I was remembering this morning? Once, when we were kids, Jason built a secret tunnel. It was part of an old lava tunnel, and it was nearly fifty feet long—it went from our backyard to right near Waikiki Beach. We'd use it to sneak to the beach and then we'd build sand castles. After a while we'd take the tunnel home again. Mom and Dad wouldn't even know that we'd left the house. And they never found out about the tunnel, either.

GW: PERHAPS THE TEAM WOULD LIKE TO SEE THE TUNNEL.

ROB: Well, they'd have to travel five thousand miles. Waikiki Beach is in Hawaii. My family used to live there. We've lived in lots of different places: Wyoming, New Jersey, California—and I was born in Texas. Dad was in the air force, so we've been stationed at military bases all around the country.

GW: IT SOUNDS EXCITING!

ROB: Really? I don't know. I think it's more exciting to stay in one place and have . . .

GW: HAVE WHAT?

ROB: Oh, never mind. Yeah, when you think about it, I guess living in all of those places was kind of neat.

GW: WHICH WAS YOUR FAVORITE PLACE?

ROB: That's a tough one. I liked California because of the giant redwood trees they have there. Some of those trees were so big, you could build four-lane highways through them. But I also liked New Jersey, mostly because Walt Whitman lived there.

GW: WALT WHITMAN—A GREAT POET!

ROB: Some of his stuff I don't get. But the parts that I do understand are beautiful. He talked about *everything*—about the Civil War, and politics, and death, and beauty. Walt Whitman was deep.

GW: YOU'RE DEEP, TOO.

ROB: Yeah, unfortunately. At least that's what my dad would say.

GW: WHY?

ROB: Well, he's not much into my poetry. I think he'd be more proud of me if I hit a baseball over a fence or scored a goal in hockey. But *I'm* not much into that stuff. He and I don't agree on a lot of things.

GW: WHY NOT?

ROB: I don't know—we just don't. He'll say fat, I'll say skinny. He'll say hot, I'll say cold. We're just different people, that's all.

GW: IS THAT A BAD THING?

ROB: When you're living under the same roof with someone really different from you, it's not the greatest thing. But I'd rather not talk about it.

GW: A GENTLEMAN NAMED MARK TWAIN ONCE SAID SOMETHING THAT YOU MIGHT FIND INTERESTING.

ROB: Mark Twain? Now *he* was a great writer!

He wrote *The Adventures of Huckleberry Finn* and *The Adventures of Tom Sawyer*. What did he say?

GW: HE SAID, "WHEN I WAS A BOY OF FOURTEEN, MY FATHER WAS SO IGNORANT I COULD HARDLY STAND TO HAVE THE OLD MAN AROUND. BUT WHEN I GOT TO BE TWENTY-ONE, I WAS ASTONISHED AT HOW MUCH HE HAD LEARNED IN SEVEN YEARS."

ROB: Yeah. Well, that may have been true for Mark Twain, but I don't think it will be true for me.

GW: KEEP AN OPEN MIND.

ROB: I guess so. Look, Ghostwriter, I want to get started on my letter.

GW: ALL RIGHT.

ROB: Ghostwriter?

GW: YES?

ROB: Do you really think my dad will get smarter by the time I'm twenty-one?

GW: MAYBE. IF YOU HELP HIM LEARN.

ROB: I think I get what you're talking about. You know, Ghostwriter, you're pretty deep yourself.

GW: THANK YOU.

ROB: Anytime. Catch you later.

TODD ALEXANDER

If you happen to be in suburban New Jersey one Saturday morning and a bunch of guys on skates go zipping by, try to get a good look at them. The one wearing the weird T-shirt and the funky-looking cap just might be *Ghostwriter*'s Todd Alexander (Rob). Chances are, Todd and his buddies are doing one of the things they like to do best: Rollerblading.

"We blade all over the place," Todd says. "There's an industrial park near my house, and on the weekends no one works there, so we go there. There are a lot of loading ramps and stuff. It's great!"

When he's not working, Todd likes to spend as much time as he can with his friends. But *Ghostwriter* is a full-time job. Todd's very busy—

especially for someone who got into acting by accident!

Here's how it happened: Todd's older brother and sister, Jeremy and Emily, were the actors in his family. They'd been acting since before Todd was born. Whenever they had auditions, their mother had to take them. And who would come tagging along? Todd.

Todd wasn't too impressed with acting, but one day his mom heard about a commercial that four-year-old Todd might be good for. He went to the audition and got the part. The commercial was for Jell-O, and he got a chance to work with Jell-O spokesman Bill Cosby. And he had fun! "It was in Lake Tahoe, and I thought, Hey, this is great. You get free trips!"

But the longer Todd stayed in show business, the tougher things got. For a while he even thought of giving it up. "It was hard because you can't really have much of a social life when you're going out on auditions every day," he says now. "But you have to make choices, I guess."

It's lucky for *Ghostwriter* that Todd's choice was to keep on acting. And Todd says *he's* glad about it, too. "Acting is a part of me," he says. "I've been doing it forever."

Todd's brother and sister aren't doing as much acting as Todd is these days. Jeremy works in Washington, D.C., and Emily is in college—also in Washington, D.C. When they all lived together, Todd says, the kids didn't always get along so well. They fought over typical things, like messing with each other's stuff and what to watch on television. Todd admits that sometimes he'd get away with murder. "Being the youngest one, everything bad I did got blamed on them," he says with a smile. "The youngest one never gets blamed, right?"

Now that they're all older, have things changed between Jeremy, Emily, and Todd? A little. "When I go and visit them, they're kind of nice—but after a while we get back into fighting and stuff," says Todd. He laughs. "You know, normal."

When Todd was young, his parents divorced. He now lives with his mom. The two are very close. It's a good thing, because they spend lots of time together!

Each day Mrs. Cohen drives Todd to the studio in Manhattan. At the end of the day the two of them might check out a museum before heading home to New Jersey. On weekends they sometimes go to street festivals or food fairs in Manhattan. There's a small shop in Manhattan where Todd likes to buy T-shirts.

T-shirts and caps are Todd's style. Especially caps. When he finds a cap he likes, he grows attached to it. The cap becomes almost like a friend.

For a long time Todd had a cap made of African kente cloth. He wore it every single day. Then the worst happened. "It ripped, and my mom made me throw it out," he says. "It was very emotional. I had it for, like, three years. So I threw it out and found a new hat. That's the one that I have now. It says JIVE FRESH on it."

Todd is on the lookout for a new cap again, though. The back of his present cap is breaking. It's no wonder, when you think about how much Todd wears that cap. The only places you'll see him without it are on the set of *Ghostwriter* and in school.

Mention school to Todd and you're likely to

get a groan. He likes to learn, but he isn't crazy about school. And he *really* isn't crazy about math. "It doesn't come to me as easily as I want it to," Todd says. "It's one of the only classes that I really have to study hard for."

Even though he complains, Todd does well in school. He's in many advanced and honors classes. What's the secret of his success? Well, he likes a challenge. And it probably also has something to do with one of his favorite activities—reading.

Like many of the actors on *Ghostwriter,* Todd loves to read. His room has two bookshelves filled with books. He likes Sherlock Holmes and science fiction books, especially those by Harry Harrison. His favorite book, though, was one called *The Charm School*. It is about the United States and the Soviet Union. "I guess it's kind of outdated now," Todd says, "but it was a really good book."

Another one of Todd's favorite activities is collecting autographed baseballs. "My mom went to a flea market and bought me this frame with an autographed picture of Mickey Mantle in it," Todd says. "It had a case under it, and I put my Mickey Mantle autographed ball in it."

Besides Mickey Mantle, Todd has baseballs signed by Will Clark, Rickey Henderson, Eric Davis, Jose Canseco, Bob Feller, and Dwight Gooden. He keeps all of these baseballs in little holders in his bedroom. But if you go to Todd's room, that probably won't be the first thing you'll notice. More likely you'll notice his bed. His *waterbed*.

"I asked for one for, like, ten years, and finally my mom got me one for my twelfth birthday," says Todd. "I like it to be really warm in the winter. My bed's great because when I get in it, it's already warm."

If you want to be friends with Todd, it helps if you're up-to-date on current events. "I really can't stand it when people don't know what's happening in their own world," he says. "There are some kids who are just totally on another planet, and I can't talk to them for more than two minutes without going crazy."

Todd likes girls who are outgoing and who have a sense of humor. And guess what else he likes—cooking!

"Mostly I just cook brownies and stuff—and

cookies—but I also like to make tacos and chicken and macaroni and cheese," he says. "And when my mom's having a dinner party, I'll help her out."

But Todd isn't *all* serious. He likes lots of things besides cooking and current events and reading. Like Bugs Bunny and Road Runner cartoons. And telling silly jokes. And going to the arcade at the mall and playing Rampart, his favorite video game.

Since Todd's character, Rob, was the last person to join the Ghostwriter team, Todd was the last actor to join the show. The other actors—Blaze, Sheldon, David, Mayteana, and Tram-anh—had known one another for a while. But it didn't take long for Todd to fit right in. "We get along," Todd says of his co-workers. "We have our tiffs, but I think we all don't mind each other. This is a really cool place to be."

MORE FUN-FILLED GHOSTWRITER BOOKS

☐ **A MATCH OF WILLS** — 29934-4
by Eric Weiner — $2.99/$3.50 in Canada

☐ **THE GHOSTWRITER DETECTIVE GUIDE:** — 48069-3
Tools and Tricks of the Trade
by Susan Lurie — $2.99/$3.50 in Canada

☐ **COURTING DANGER AND OTHER STORIES** — 48070-7
by Dina Anastasio — $2.99/$3.50 in Canada

☐ **DRESS CODE MESS** — 48071-5
by Sara St. Antoine — $2.99/$3.50 in Canada

☐ **THE BIG BOOK OF KIDS' PUZZLES** — 37074-X
by P.C. Russell Ginns — $1.25/$1.50 in Canada

☐ **THE MINI BOOK OF KIDS' PUZZLES** — 37073-1
by Denise Lewis Patrick — $.99/$1.25 in Canada

☐ **OFF THE TOP OF YOUR HEAD:** — 37157-6
Trivia, Facts, and Fun
by Christina Wilsdon — $1.25/$1.50 in Canada

☐ **STEER CLEAR OF HAUNTED HILL** — 48087-1
by Eric Weiner — $2.99/$3.50 in Canada

BANTAM BOOKS
Dept. DA55, 2451 South Wolf Road, Des Plaines, IL 60018

Please send me the items I have checked above. I am enclosing
$_____ (please add $2.50 to cover postage and handling).
Send check or money order, no cash or C.O.D.'s please.

MR/MS _____

ADDRESS _____

CITY/STATE _____ ZIP _____

Please allow four to six weeks for delivery.
Prices and availability subject to change without notice. — DA55 8/93